Book Review

Fluttering Beauties is a beautiful coloring book that takes you on an adventure through the world of butterflies. The book is filled with intricate and detailed illustrations,descriptions of various activities of butterflies and their natural habitats.

Each page features a unique pattern and design, providing hours of entertainment and relaxation. Whether you're an expert colorist or just starting out, the beautiful butterfly designs in this book are sure to inspire creativity and joy. Each page invites you to unleash your creativity and bring the stunning butterflies to life with vibrant colors. The book is not only visually stunning but also informative, providing interesting facts about each butterfly throughout the book. This coloring book is perfect for all ages, offering a delightful way to reduce stress and relax while learning about the delicate beauty and ecosystem of butterflies. Overall, Fluttering Beauties is an excellent choice for those who appreciate the wonder and majesty of these stunning creatures.

Are you ready to improve on your skills? Trust me this book got you covered.

Explore A Beautiful Butterfly Adventure

Good luck on your coloring.

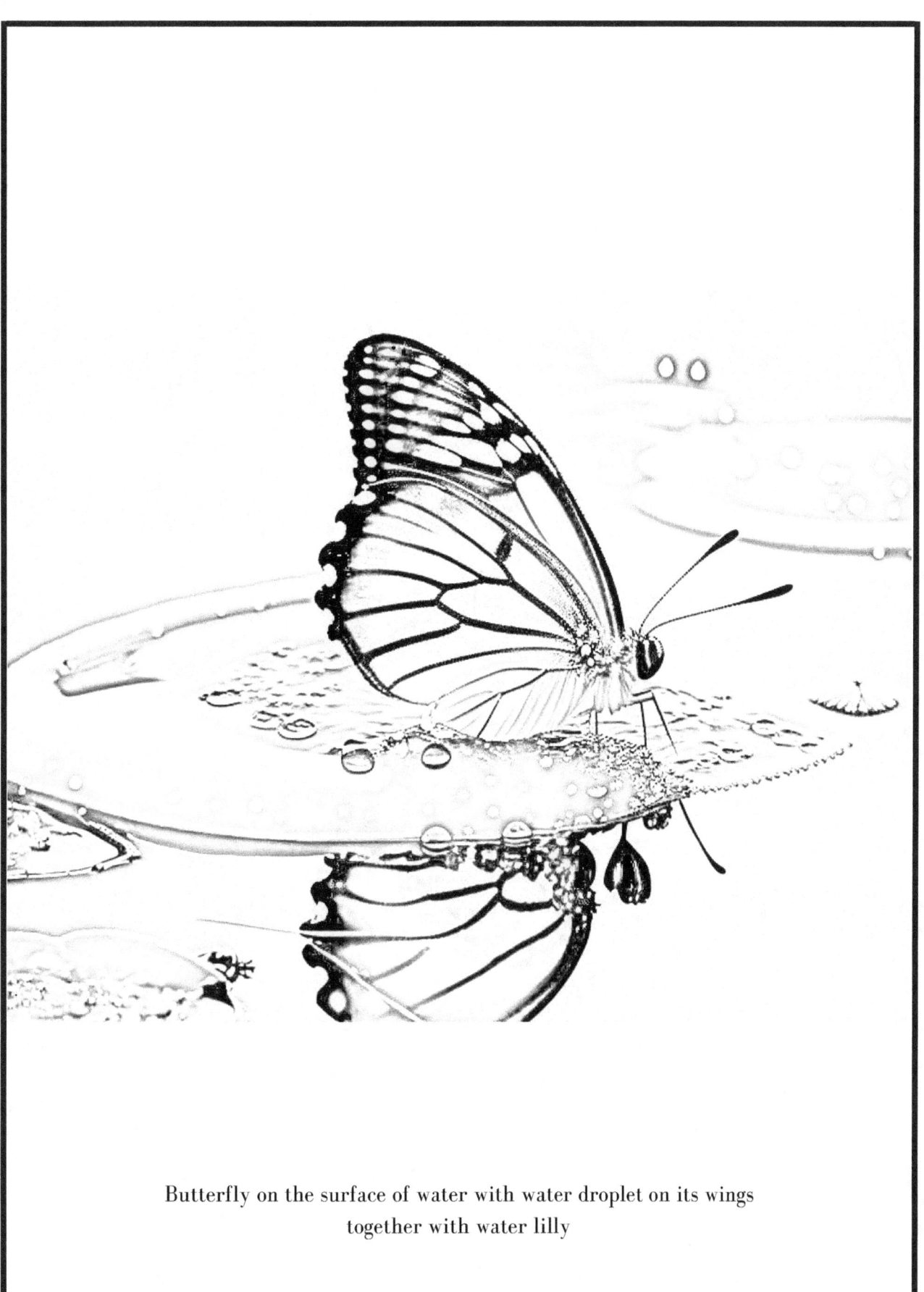

Butterfly on the surface of water with water droplet on its wings
together with water lilly

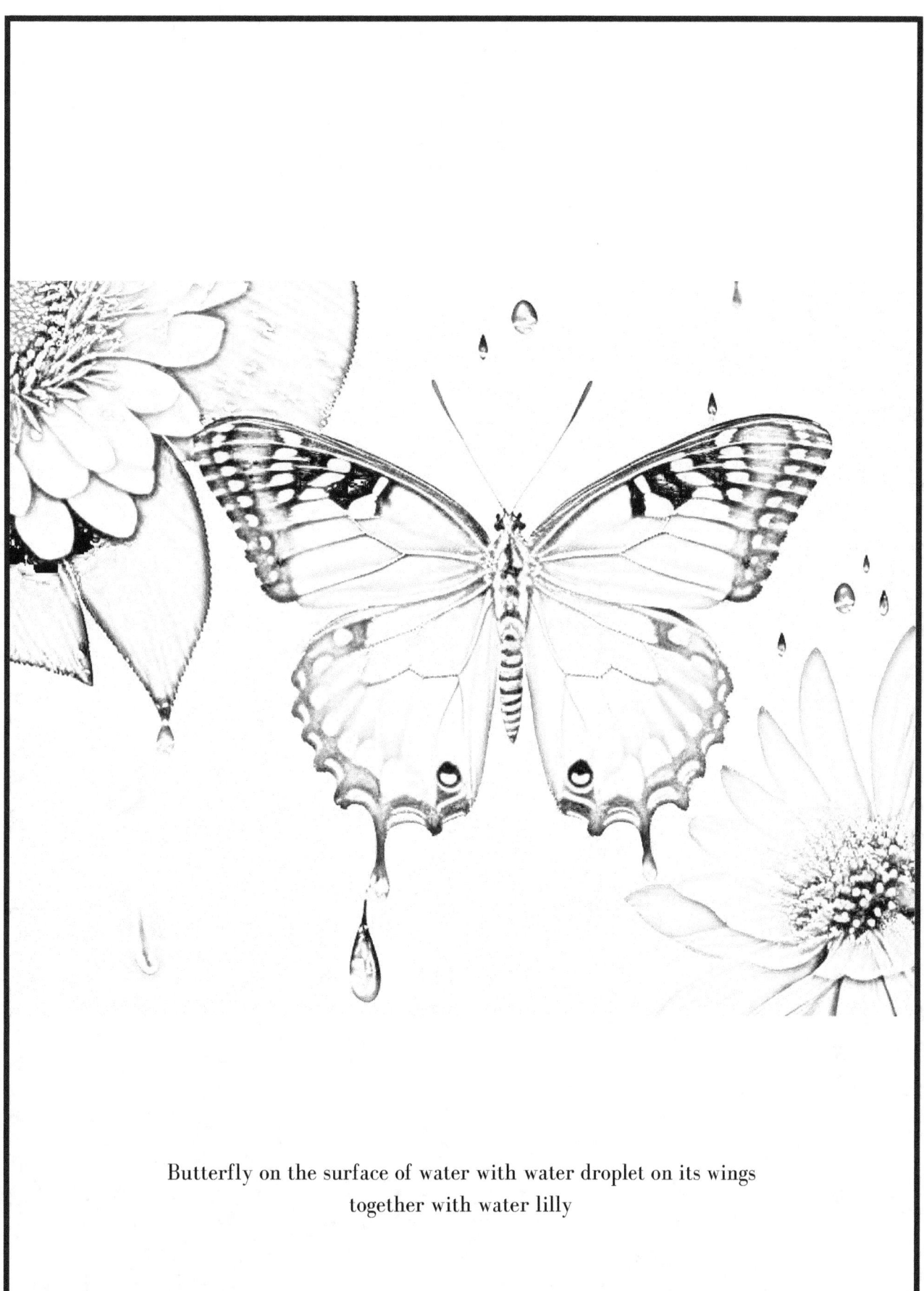

Butterfly on the surface of water with water droplet on its wings
together with water lilly

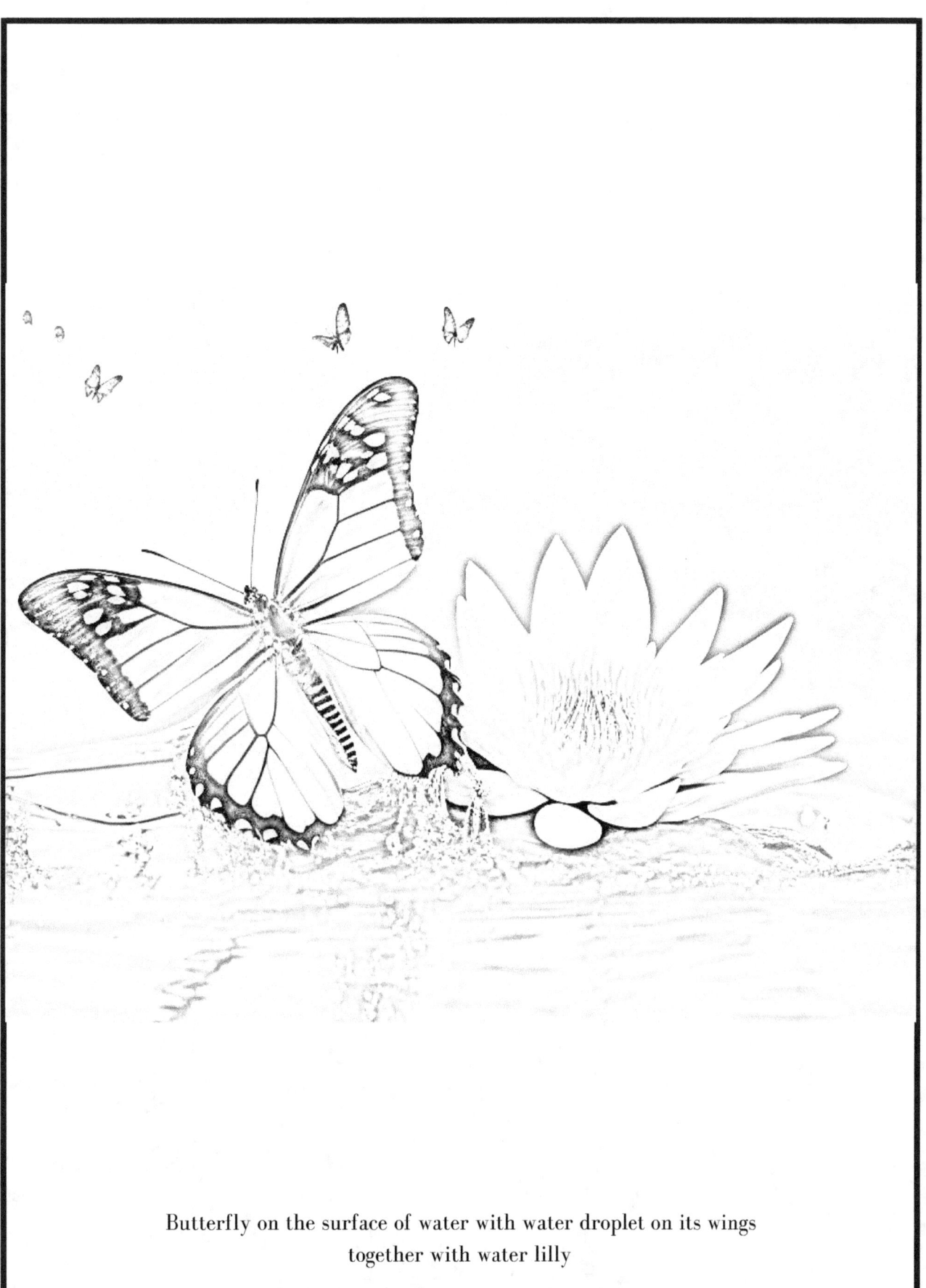

Butterfly on the surface of water with water droplet on its wings
together with water lilly

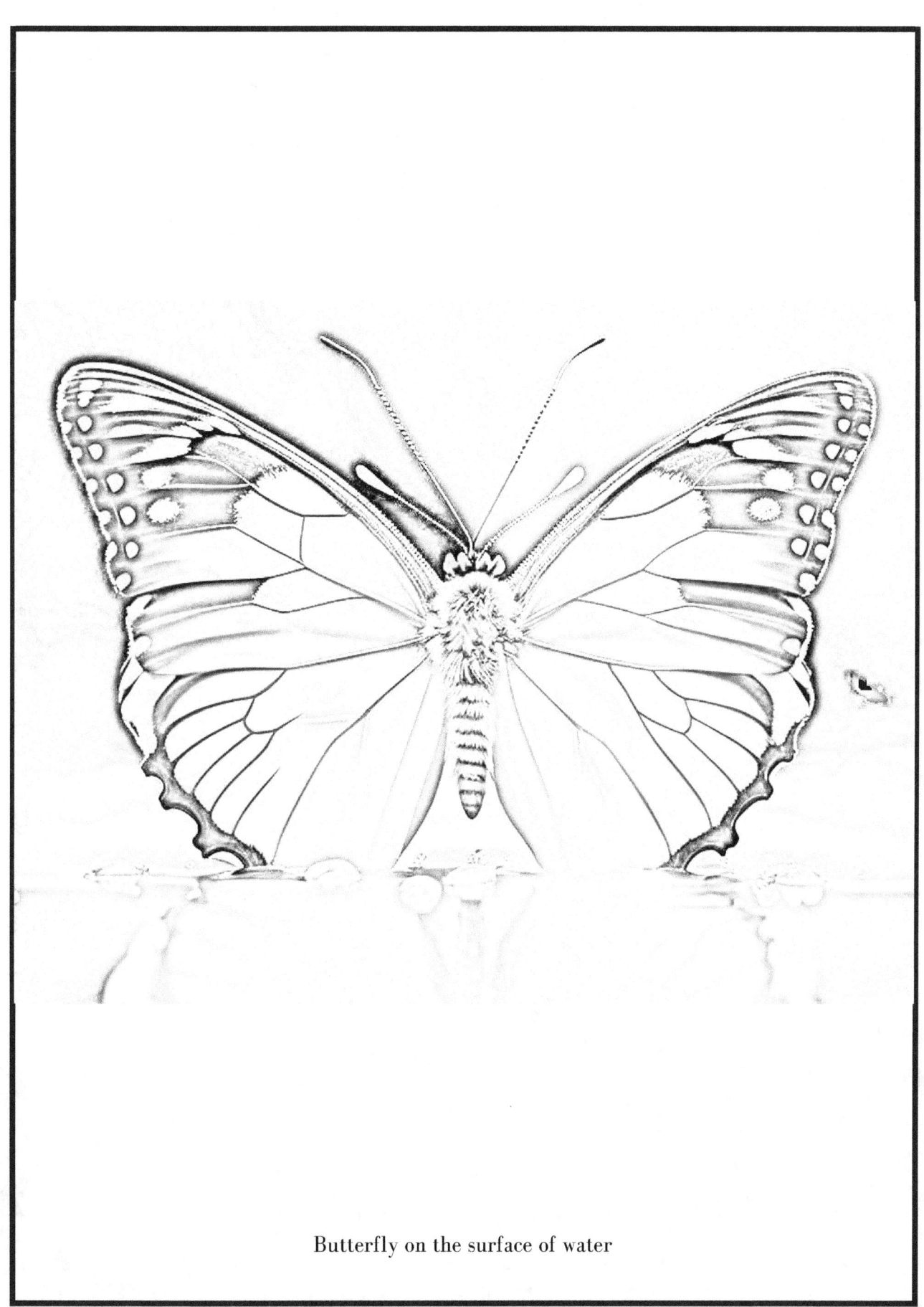

Butterfly on the surface of water

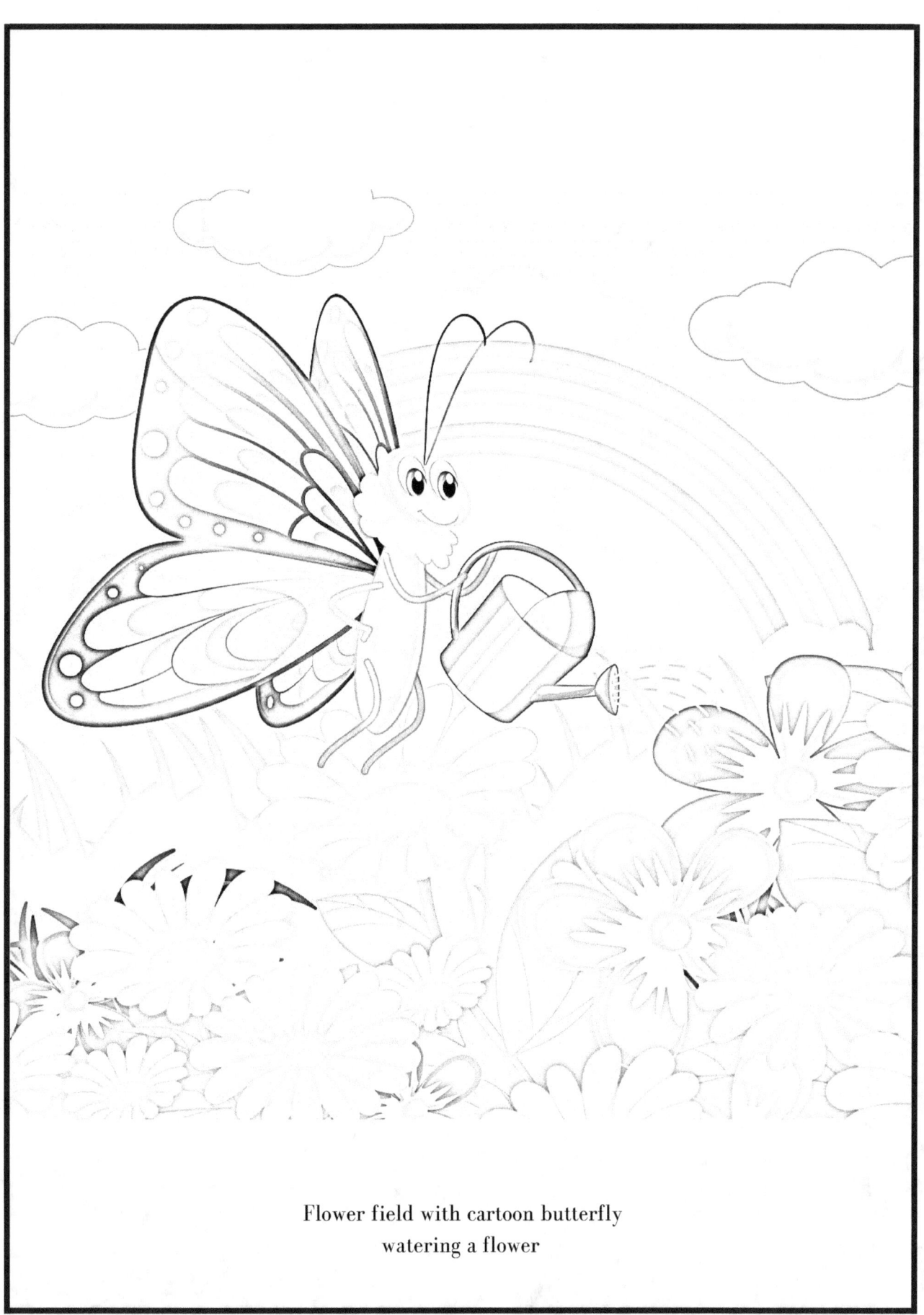

Flower field with cartoon butterfly
watering a flower

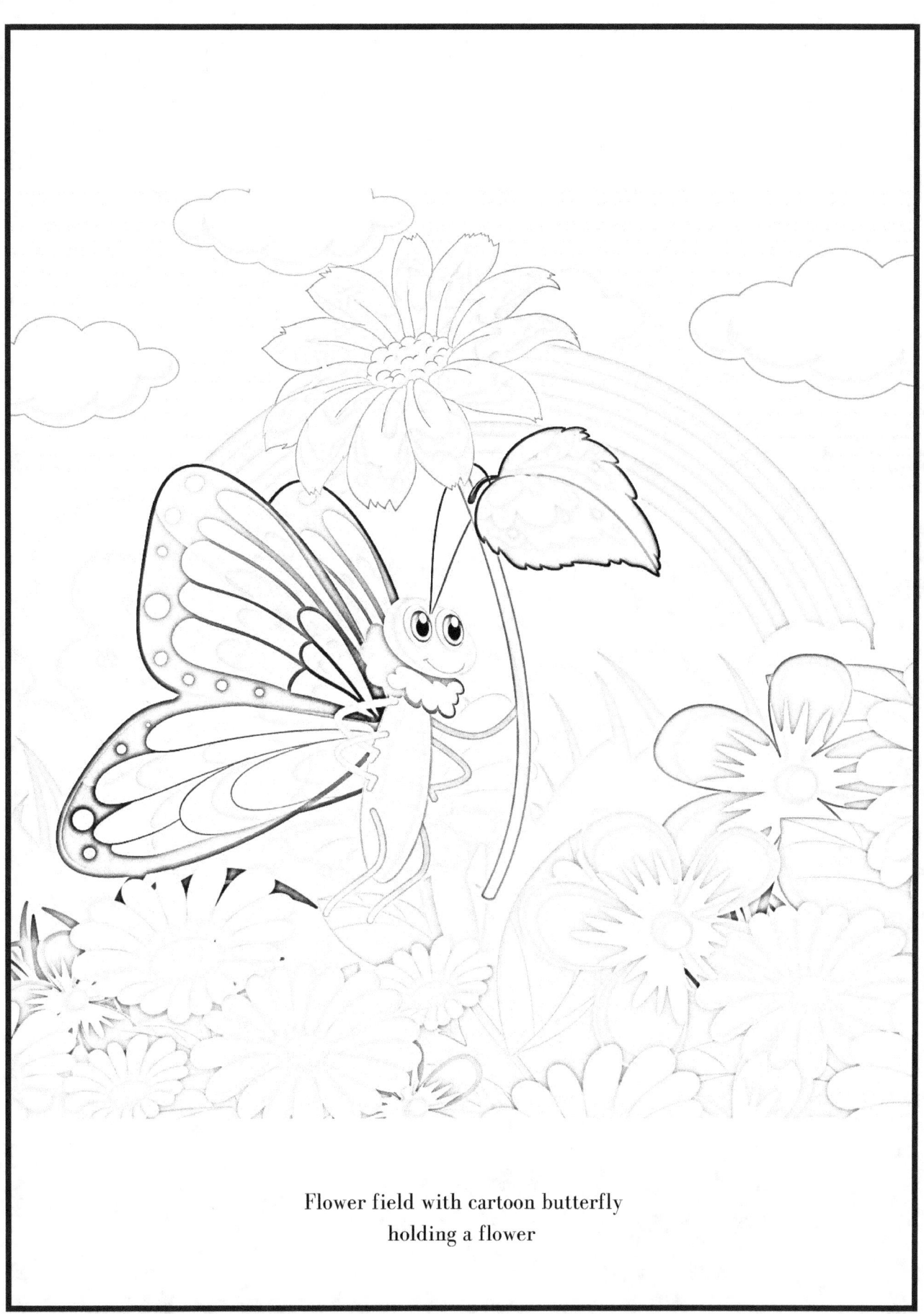

Flower field with cartoon butterfly
holding a flower

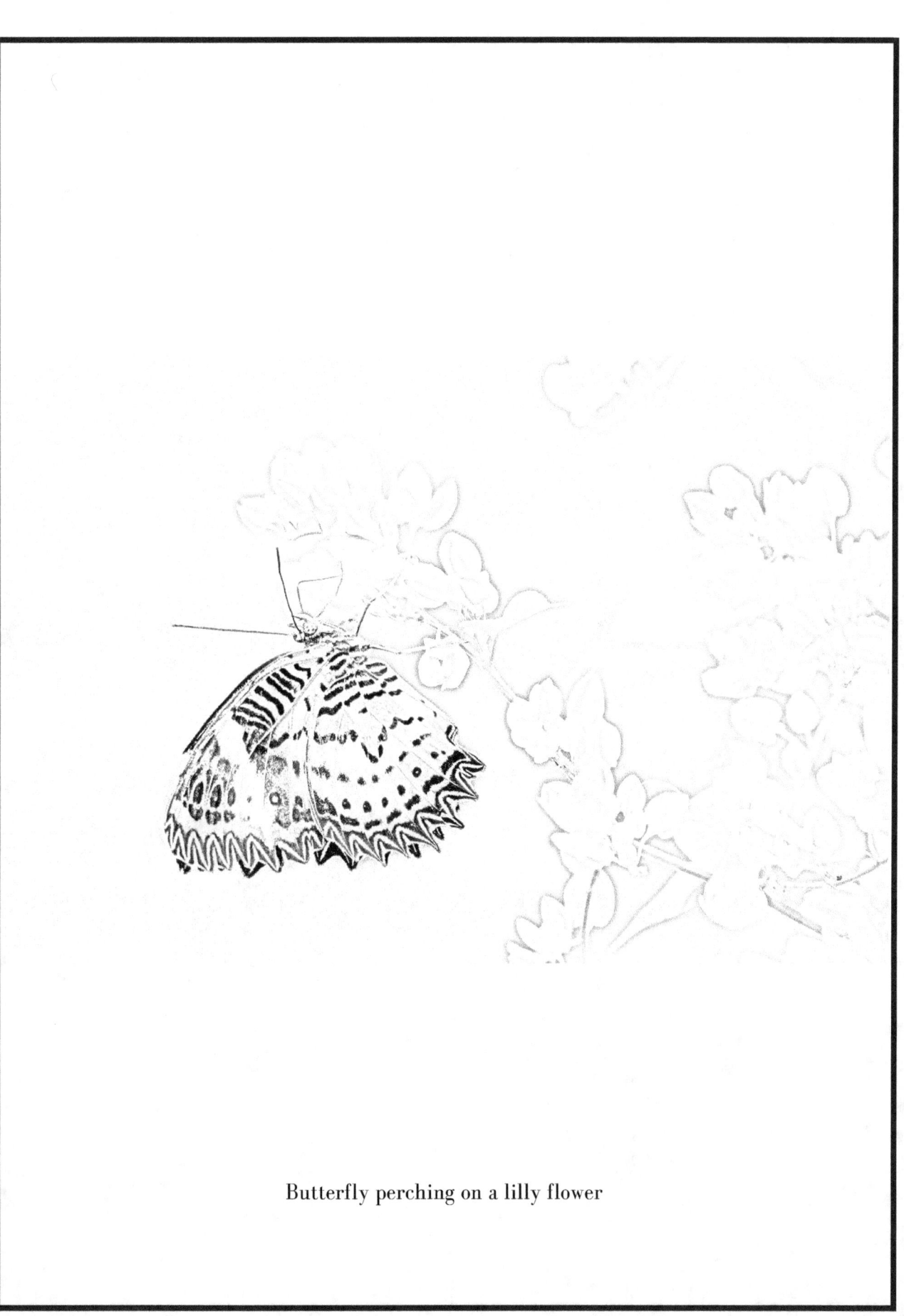

Butterfly perching on a lilly flower

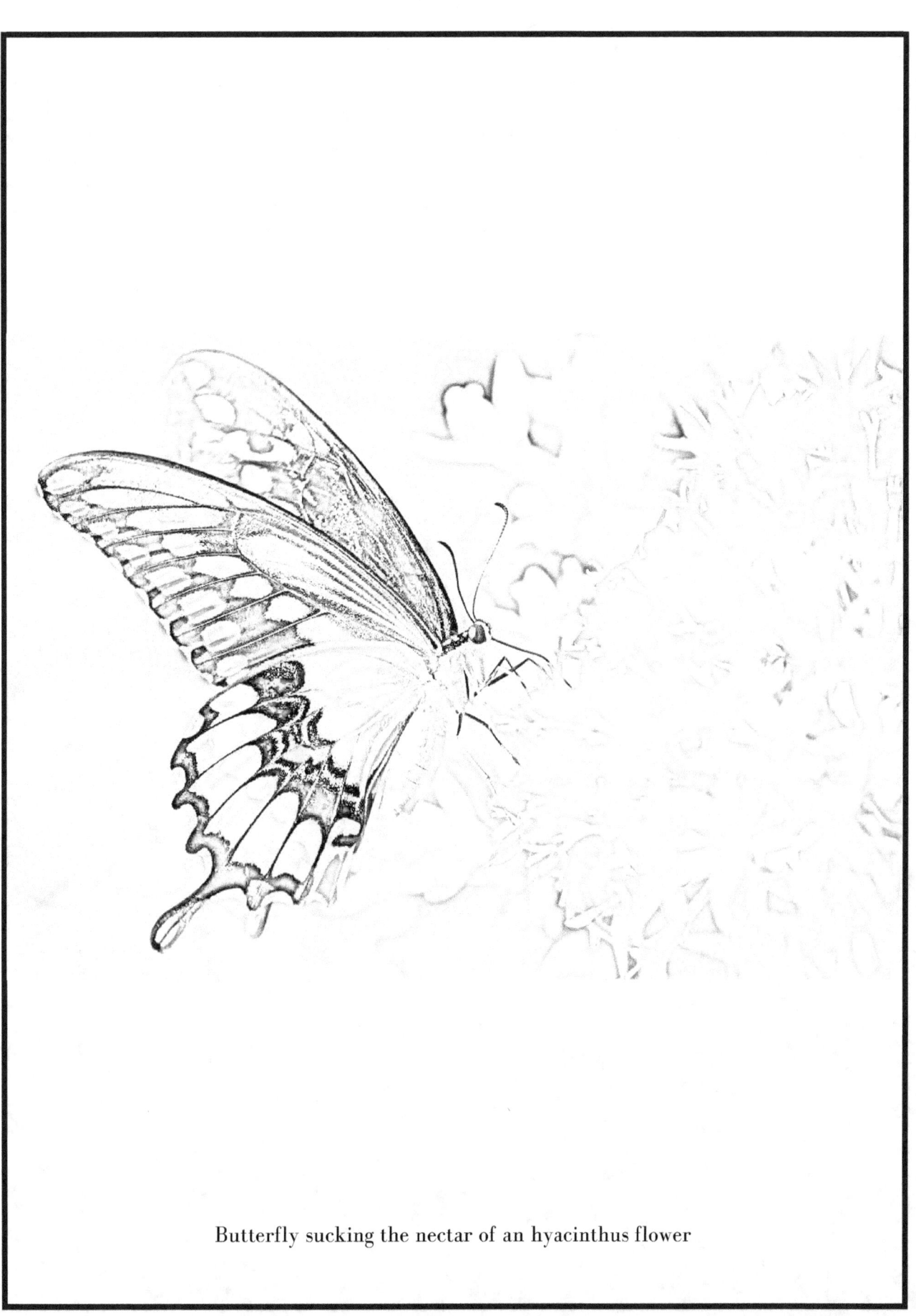

Butterfly sucking the nectar of an hyacinthus flower

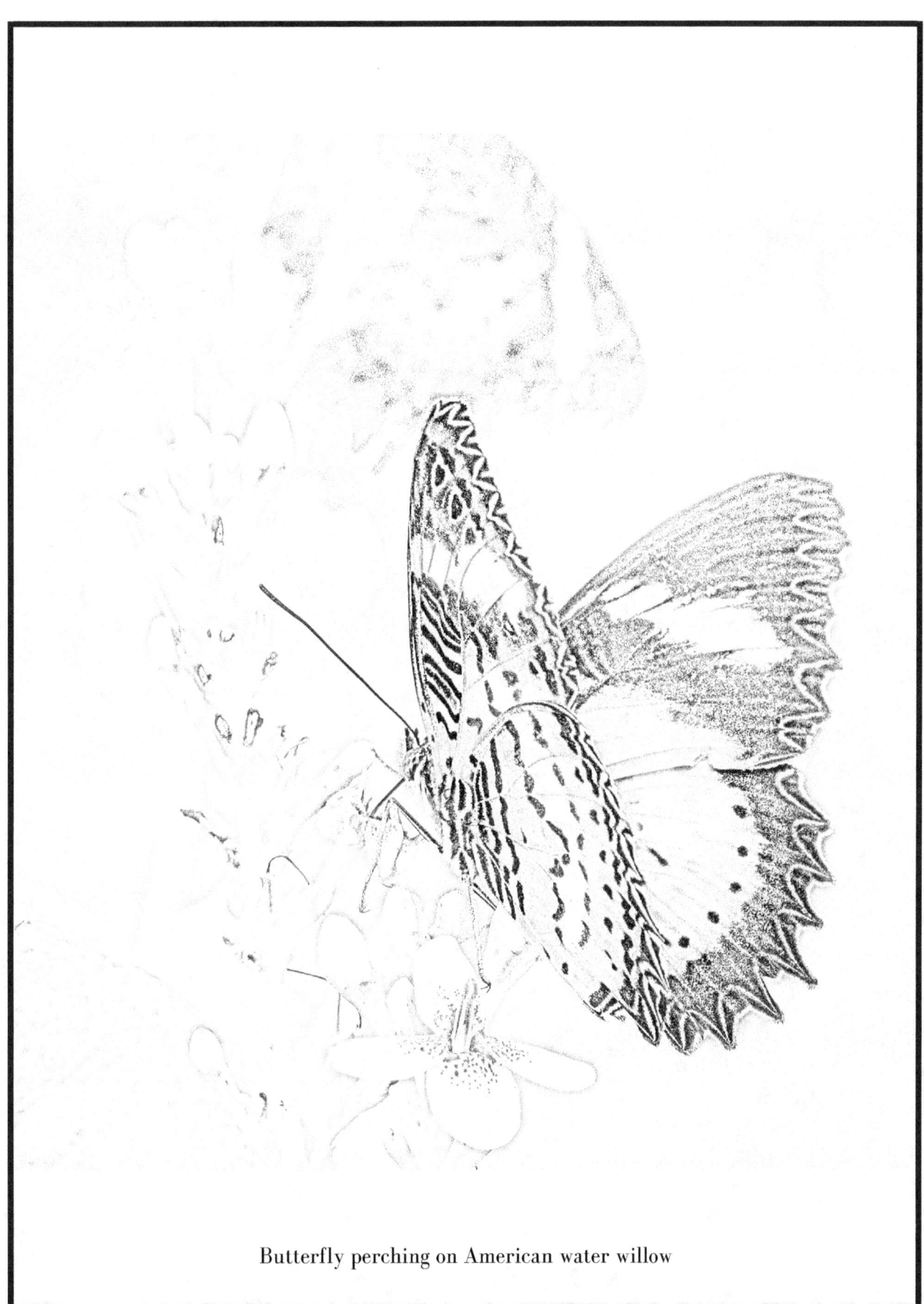

Butterfly perching on American water willow

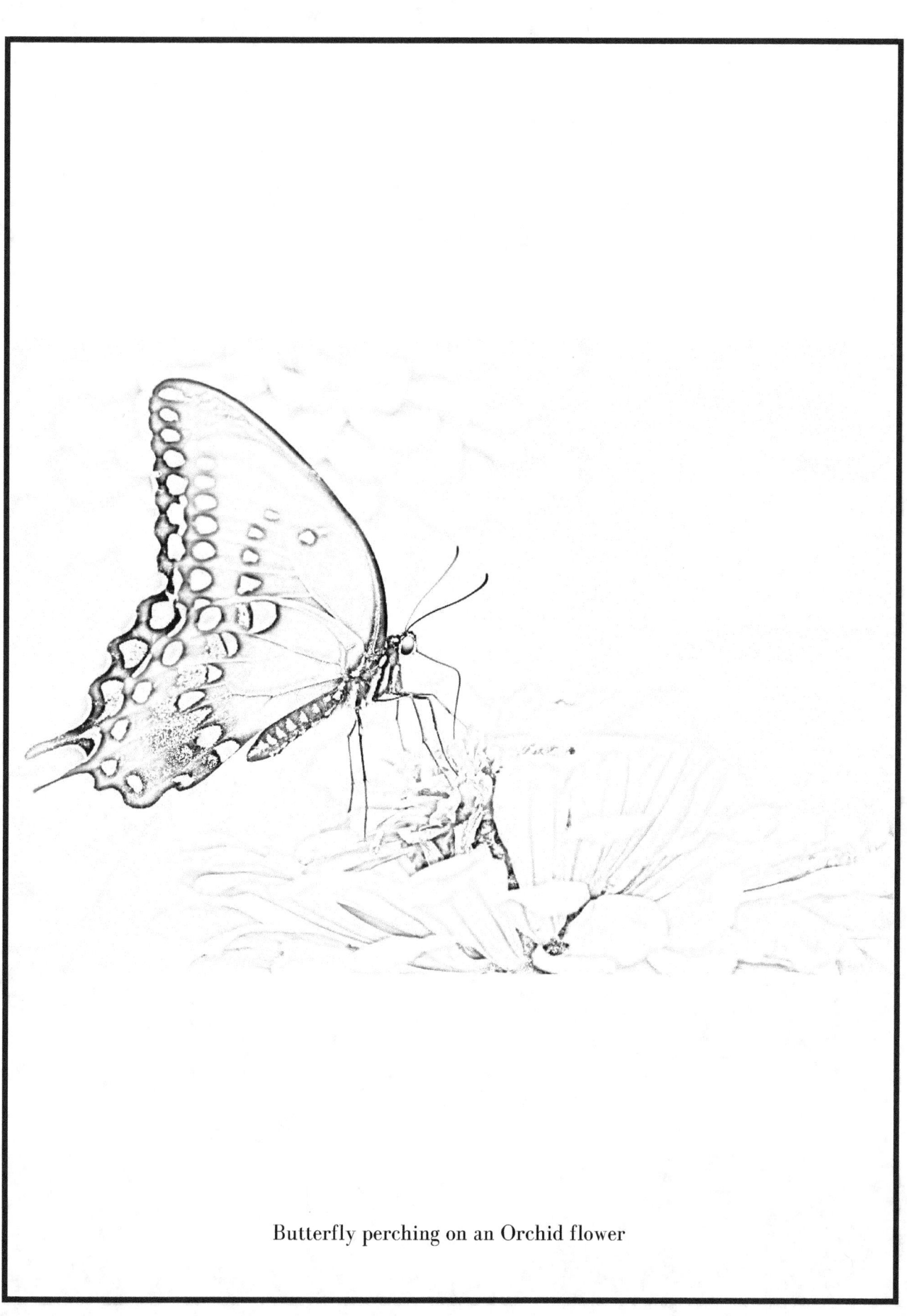

Butterfly perching on an Orchid flower

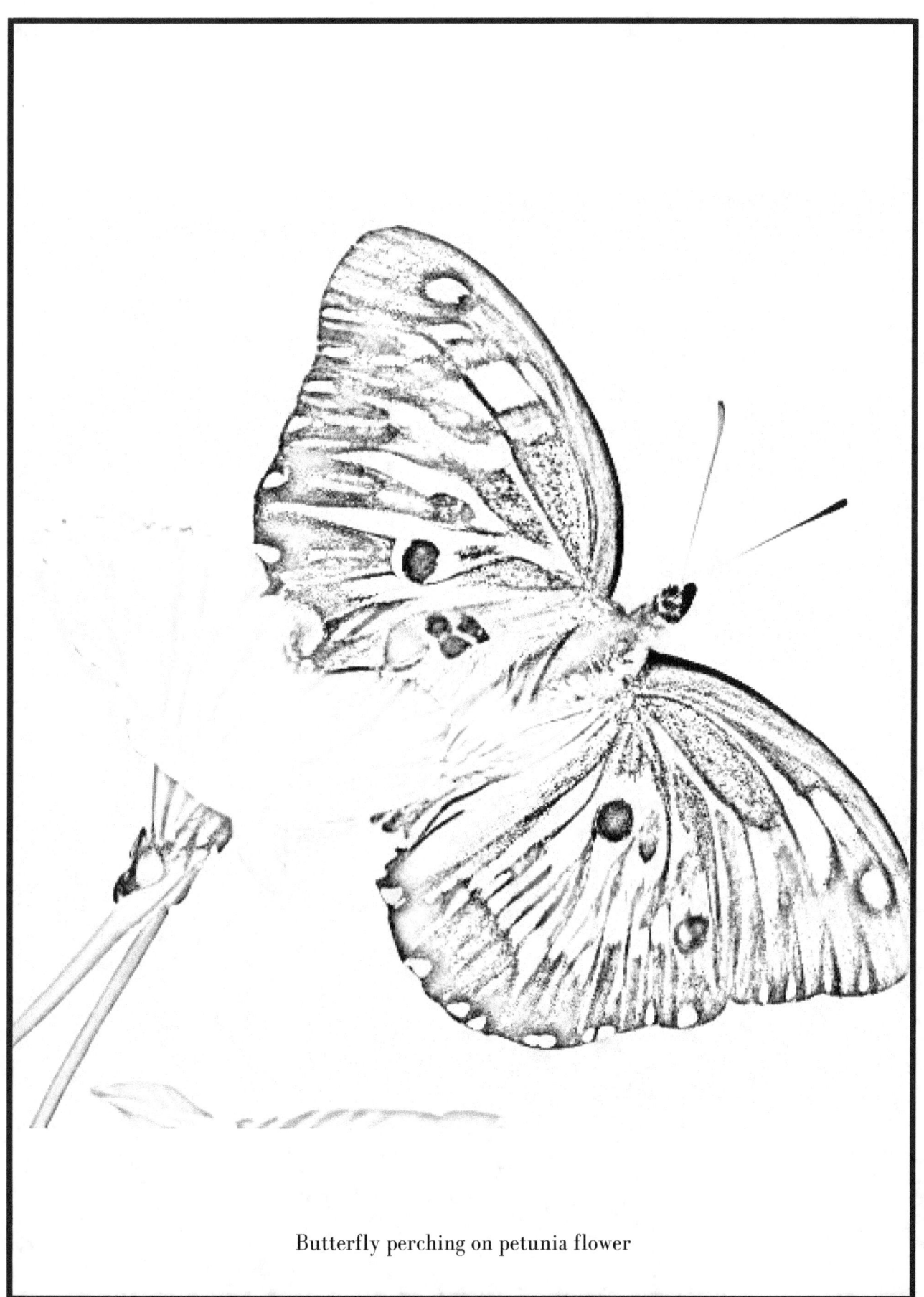

Butterfly perching on petunia flower

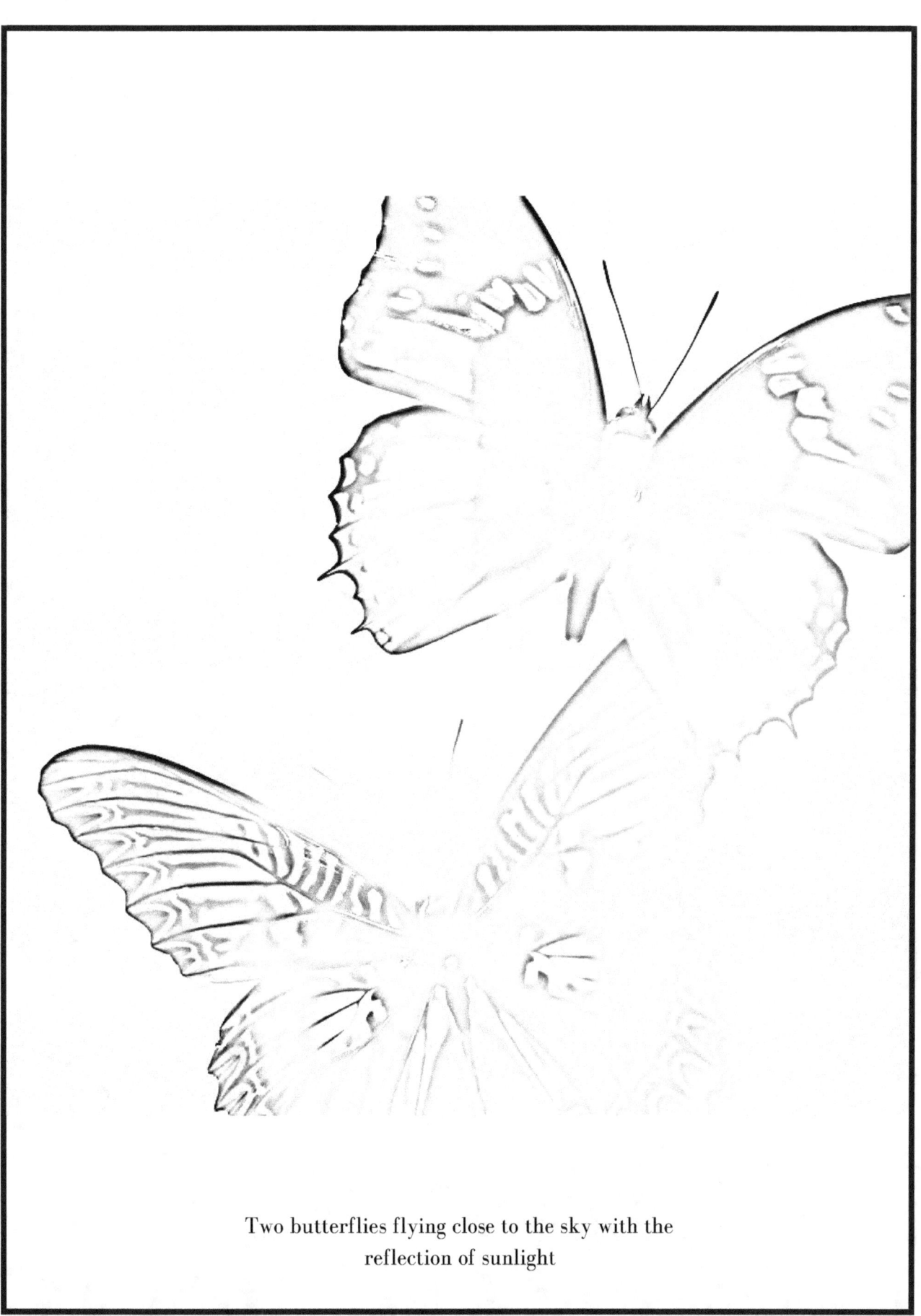

Two butterflies flying close to the sky with the
reflection of sunlight

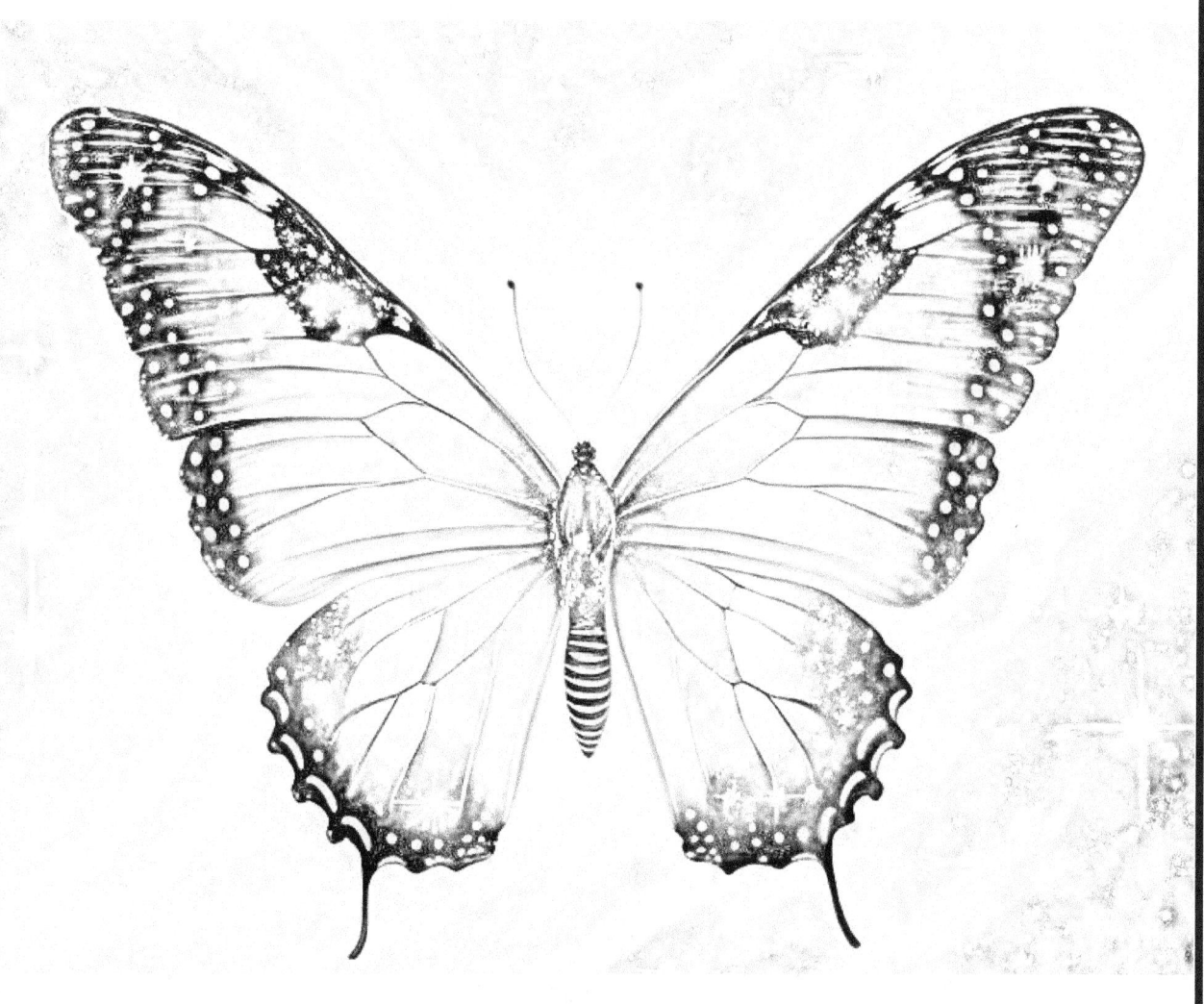

Butterfly with intricate patterns on its wings flying
through a star-filled galaxy

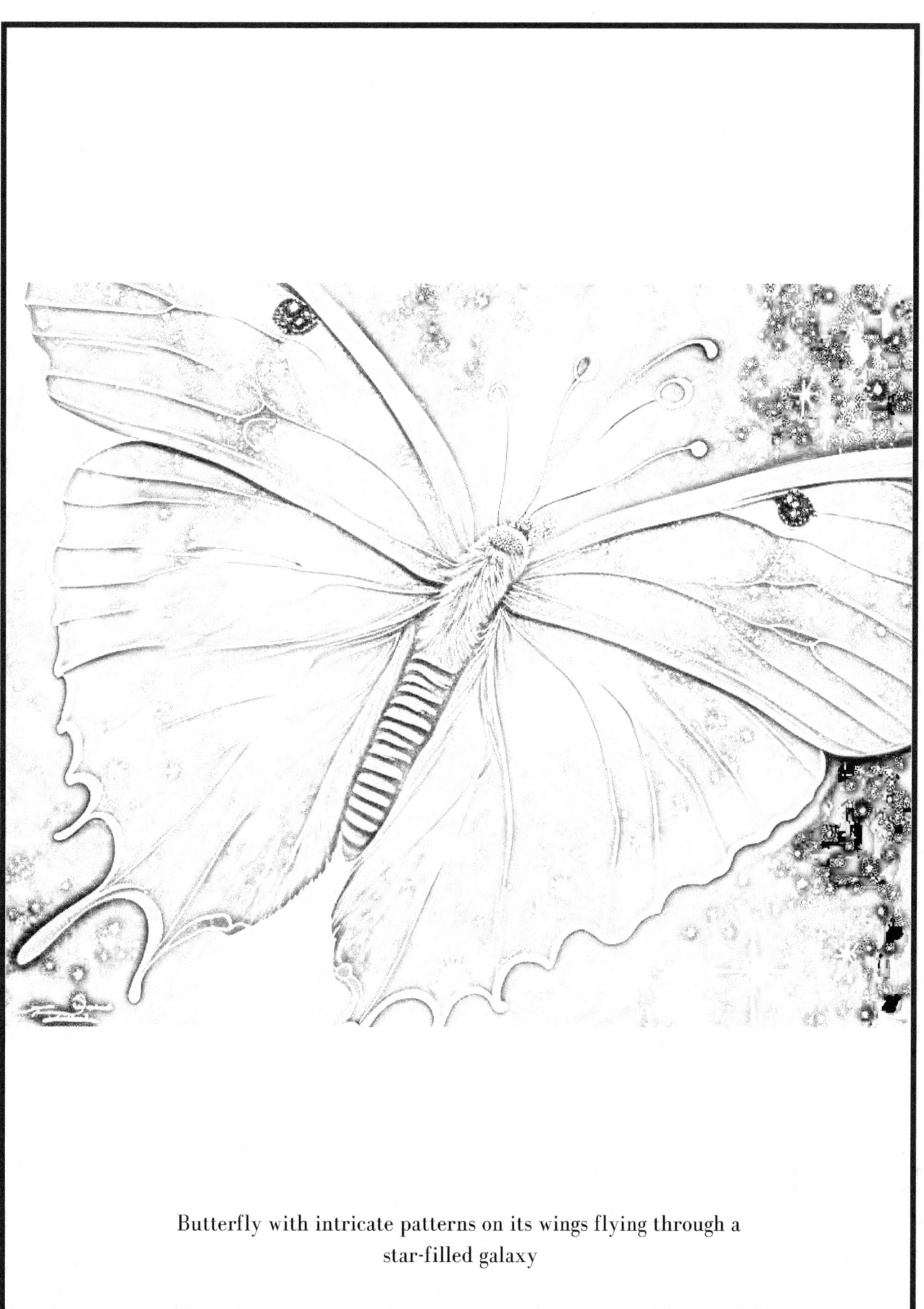

Butterfly with intricate patterns on its wings flying through a
star-filled galaxy

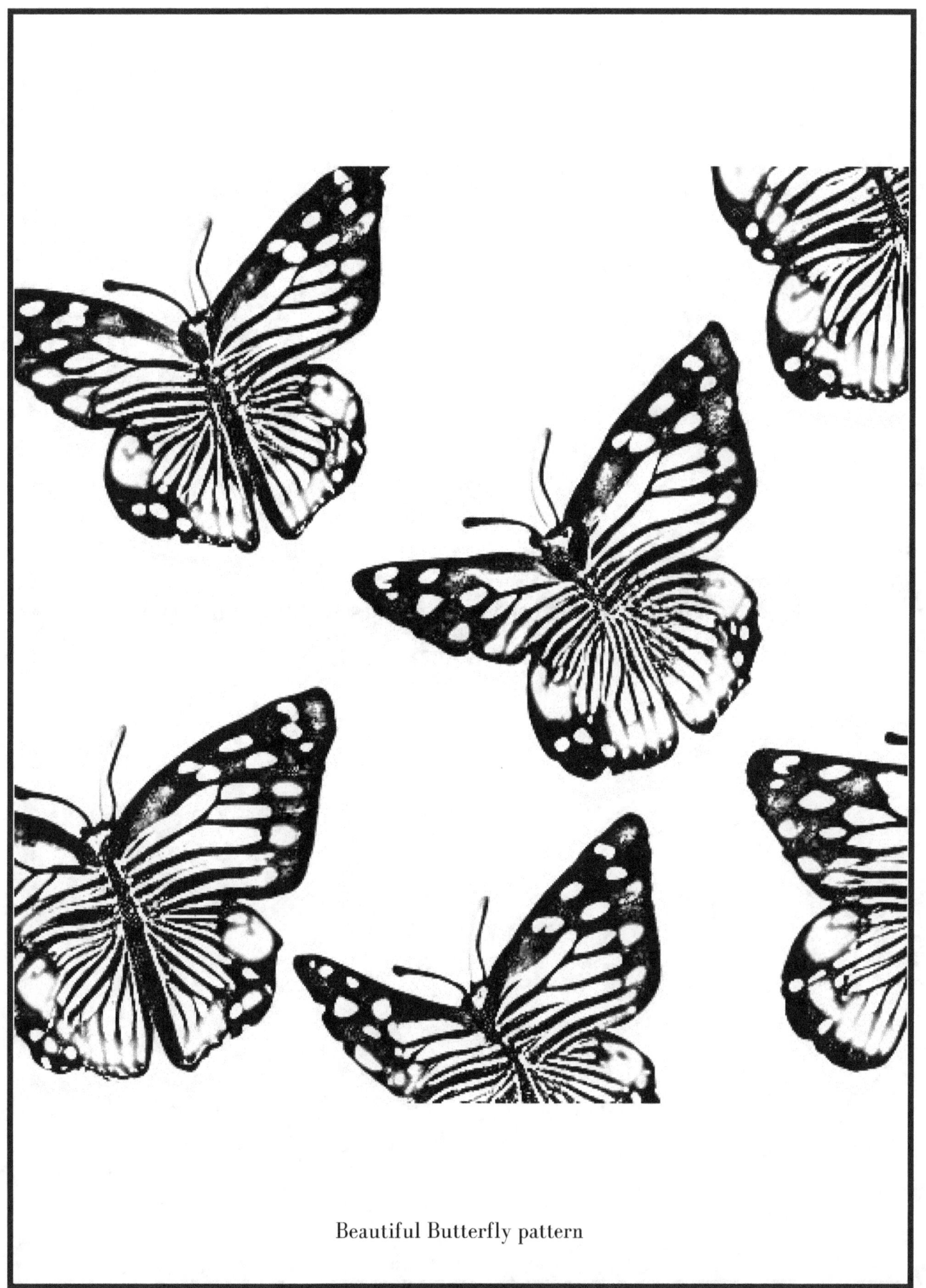

Beautiful Butterfly pattern

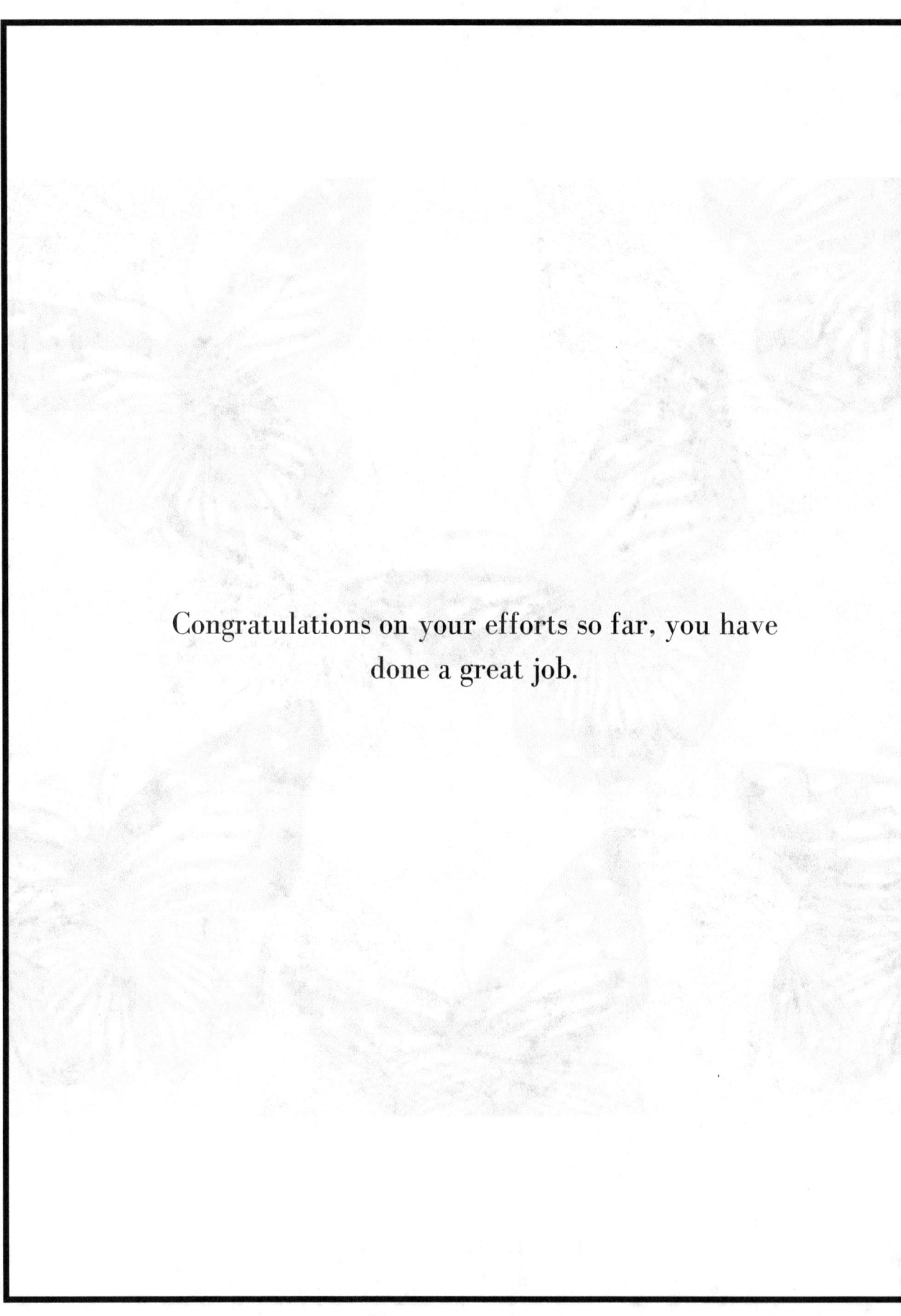

Congratulations on your efforts so far, you have
done a great job.